# ALPHABET
## DREAMS

Prentice-Hall Inc., Englewood Cliffs, N.J.

# ALPHABET DREAMS

Adapted and Illustrated by
Judith Gwyn Brown

Printed in the United States of America •J

Prentice-Hall International, Inc., London
Prentice-Hall of Australia, Pty. Ltd., North Sydney
Prentice-Hall of Canada, Ltd., Toronto
Prentice-Hall of India Private Ltd., New Delhi
Prentice-Hall of Japae, Inc., Tokyo

10  9  8  7  6  5  4  3  2  1

Library of Congress Cataloging in Publication Data

Brown, Judith Gwyn.
Alphabet dreams.

SUMMARY: An introduction to the alphabet
using the ball-bounce and jump rope rhyme, "A
My Name Is Anna."
[1. Alphabet books]   I.   Title.
PZ7.B81426Al   [E]   76-12452
ISBN 0-13-022806-0

Printed in the United States of America ·J

For Harold

# A My name is Anna,
## and my husband's name is Andrew.

We live in an aquarium,
and we sell apples.

**B** My name is Barbara,
and my husband's name is Ben.

We live in a bakery,
and we sell buns.

**C** My name is Carrie,
and my husband's name is Carl.
We live in a castle,
and we sell cats.

**D** My name is Doris,
and my husband's name is Don.
We live under a dome,
and we sell dreams.

E My name is Ellie,
and my husband's name is Ed.

We live on an elephant,
and we sell eggs.

**F** My name is Frances,
and my husband's name is Fred.
We live on a flagpole,
and we sell fireworks.

**G** My name is Gloria,
and my husband's name is George.
We live in a garden,
and we sell grapes.

**H** My name is Helen,
and my husband's name is Hal.
We live near a hive,
and we sell honey.

**I** My name is Irene,
and my husband's name is Ike.
We live on an island,
and we sell ices.

**J** My name is Juanita,
and my husband's name is Jack.
We live in a jug,
and we sell jewels.

**K** My name is Kathy,
and my husband's name is Ken.
We live in a kettle,
and we sell kites.

**L** My name is Lucy,
and my husband's name is Lee.
We live in a log,
and we sell lamps.

**M** My name is Maggie,
and my husband's name is Max.
We live on a mountain,
and we sell mugs.

**N** My name is Nina,
and my husband's name is Ned.
We live in a nest,
and we sell nuts.

O My name is Olga,
and my husband's name is Owen.
We live at the opera,
and we sell organs.

**P** My name is Patty,
and my husband's name is Pete.
We live in a park,
and we sell paint.

**Q** My name is Queenie,
and my husband's name is Quint.
We live on a quilt,
and we sell quills.

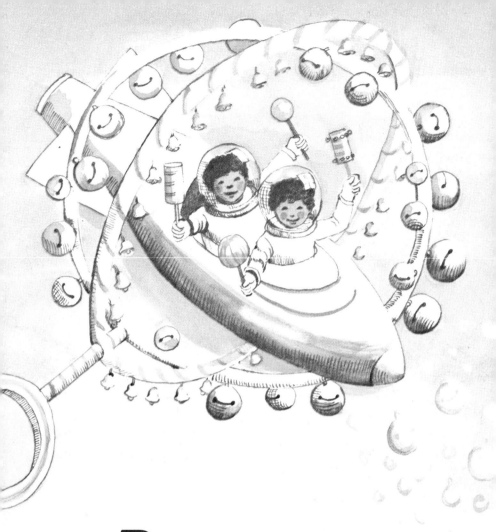

**R** My name is Rosie,
and my husband's name is Ralph.
We live in a rocket,
and we sell rattles.

**S** My name is Susan,
and my husband's name is Sam.
We live on a ship,
and we sell shells.

**T** My name is Terry,
and my husband's name is Tom.
We live in a tower,
and we sell tea.

**U** My name is Una,
and my husband's name is Ugo.
We live under an umbrella,
and we sell upholstery.

**V** My name is Violet,
and my husband's name is Val.
We live in the village,
and we sell violins.

**W** My name is Winnie,
and my husband's name is Will.
We live on a wagon,
and we sell wigs.

**X** My name's Xantippe, and my husband's name is **Y**ou!!!

We swing on the signs of the **Z**odiac zoo.